the
ideal
planner

Gallery Books
An Imprint of Simon & Schuster, Inc.
1230 Avenue of the Americas
New York, NY 10020

First Gallery Books hardcover edition August 2020

GALLERY BOOKS and colophon are registered trademarks of Simon & Schuster, Inc.

For information about special discounts for bulk purchases,
please contact Simon & Schuster Special Sales at 1-866-506-1949
or business@simonandschuster.com.

The Simon & Schuster Speakers Bureau can bring authors to your live event.
For more information or to book an event, contact the Simon & Schuster Speakers Bureau
at 1-866-248-3049 or visit our website at www.simonspeakers.com.

Interior design by Lizzie Vaughan
Interior illustrations by Priscilla Witte

Manufactured in China

1   3   5   7   9   10   8   6   4   2

Library of Congress Cataloging-in-Publication Data is available.

ISBN 978-1-9821-4191-2

the ideal planner

emma chamberlain

GALLERY BOOKS

New York   London   Toronto   Sydney   New Delhi

I HAVE ALWAYS BELIEVED that an organized life leads to a happier life. When I was in the fifth grade I got my first planner, and I've been using daily planners ever since. There's something about actually writing down your tasks that makes you feel more in control. There's probably a study out there somewhere that explains why writing down your responsibilities is beneficial to your brain, but I'm too lazy to find that information. *Insert statistics that you find here, LOL.*

I've been using planners for so long that I feel like I've tried every kind that exists. The funny thing is, I've never had one I truly loved. They have always felt too structured and professional. Some have even felt cliché, with activity pages that make you self-reflect in the dullest way possible. That is why I decided to make this planner. I wanted to make one that was useful for day-to-day life, while also being fun. The organization element is clean, making it easy to use, and the activity pages are more inviting and actually enjoyable. This is the planner I have always wanted. I hope you love it as much as I do.

-Emma

Here I am in middle school, around the time that I started using a planner.

You Can't Forget
(OR ELSE!)

July	August	September
		13th me and weias 1 year

October	November	December
	19th Leia bby's Bday	

DRAW YOUR BAG

and what's in it.

Mine

- ☑ Chapstick
- ☑ Keys
- ☑ Phone
- ☑ Gum
- ☑ Cat hair
- ☑ Mixed nuts
- ☑ Makeup wipes
- ☑ Hair ties
- ☑ Tic Tacs
- ☑ Glasses

Print out a bunch of cool
photos and glue them
onto the other side of
this page to make a

MOOD BOARD.

Feel free to rip
or cut it out!

MOOD
MOOD
MOOD
MOOD

2021

Year

Thursday	Friday	Saturday	
7	8	9	**NOTES**
14	15	16	
covidtest 21	22	23	
pre-recitation work due - 8:30am 28	hs quiz due 29	30	

January
_____
Month

2021
_____
Year

Notes:

◯ Monday
_____
_____
_____
_____
_____

◯ Tuesday
_____
_____
_____
_____
_____

◯ Wednesday
_____
_____
_____
_____
_____

Thursday

Friday

Take a nap today!

Saturday

Sunday

Month | **Year**

Notes:

Monday

Tuesday

Wednesday

Thursday

Friday

Saturday

Sunday

Month

Year

Notes:

Monday

_____

_____

_____

_____

_____

Tuesday

_____

_____

_____

_____

_____

Wednesday

_____

_____

_____

_____

_____

Thursday

Friday

Saturday

Sunday

Month   **Year**

Notes:

Monday

Tuesday

Wednesday

Thursday

Friday

Saturday

Sunday

Month

Year

Notes:

Monday

Tuesday

Wednesday

Thursday

Friday

Saturday

Sunday

COFFEE · CROSSWORD

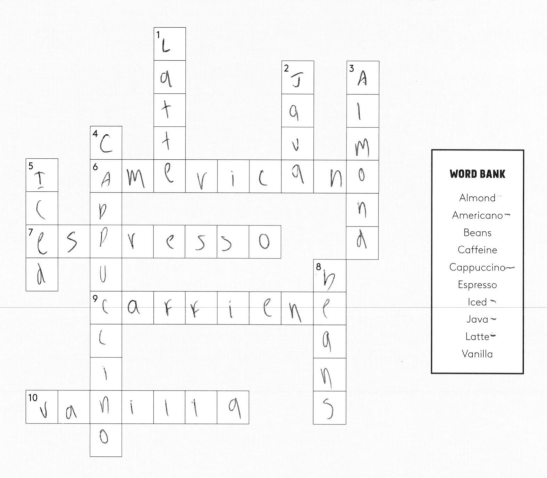

WORD BANK

Almond
Americano
Beans
Caffeine
Cappuccino
Espresso
Iced
Java
Latte
Vanilla

ACROSS

6 This is basically a black coffee, but it has a special name

7 There are two shots of this in a large latte

9 Helps keep you up when you are pulling an all-nighter

10 People who want to spice up their coffee will usually add either hazelnut, mocha, or _____ syrup

DOWN

1 Probably the most photogenic drink of them all (because of the foam-top designs)

2 Also a coding software

3 People who don't put cow's milk in their coffee often use _____ milk

4 The drink with the most foam

5 Hot coffee is okay, but _____ coffee is incredible (in my opinion, LOL)

8 These are used in making coffee, but other kinds can also give you gas

DESIGN

A

PHONE

CASE.

YOUR SIGN
WHAT IT REALLY SAYS ABOUT YOU

ARIES

For some reason Aries have to be the leaders of every situation they are in. LIKE WE GET IT!!! YOU ARE THE CAPTAIN OF THE FOOTBALL TEAM!!! OKAY!!! On the other hand, Aries have your back—they are the people who will tell you when you have food in your teeth. And we all need someone like that in our lives.

TAURUS

Somehow Taurus manages to be the funny friend, while also being the stubborn friend. A Taurus will make the best joke and then go home twenty minutes later because they are sick of everyone's bullshit. Tauruses won't be friends with just anyone; they have to trust you with their LIFE! So if you are friends with a Taurus, consider yourself special AF.

GEMINI

CRAZY BITCH ENERGY!!! Geminis have never been quiet for more than four minutes in their entire lives. Somehow Geminis manage to be dramatic and unpredictable, while also being clever, funny, and charming. Let me tell you, hanging out with a Gemini will be fun, but you may need a nap after.

CANCER

Cancers are always the artistic and nurturing ones in the group. They have an appreciation for food and art that is unmatched, but they also have an appreciation for THEMSELVES that is unmatched. They will vividly describe memories to you for an hour and wait for you to thank them when they're finished. (Their memory is really good for some reason.) Also, Cancers always win arguments, so don't even try to start with them.

LEO

THE WORLD REVOLVES AROUND LEOS, DOESN'T IT?! Although Leos would drop anything to help you fix your tire, they would also drop anything to go sing karaoke and show off their "singing skills." There is never a dull moment with a Leo. They are great people to bring around because they LOVE to be social and are very loyal. (They serve as great wingwomen/wingmen, I'm just saying.)

VIRGO

Virgos are perfectionists, which is great, but they need to RELAX! Virgos need to take a day off and go get a massage or something, seriously. They are just constantly multitasking. They're analyzing a situation that happened to them earlier, while dealing with their own thoughts, while also noticing shit that NOBODY ELSE SEES! RELAX, SUPERHERO!!!

LIBRA

Libras are like the human version of Sour Patch Kids—they are sweet, until you get them mad, and then they turn SOUR!!! Libras do not take shit from anyone. But they can also be goofy and hilarious, so it's not unlikely to have a solid laugh with a Libra. Side note: If you are planning to go to a restaurant with a Libra, never ask them what restaurant to go to. THEY CAN NEVER DECIDE!!!

SCORPIO

Low-key scary, but also low-key FUN AF! You do not want to get on a Scorpio's bad side, let me tell you. They are the type of people who would leave a 1-star Yelp review even if it deserved 3 stars, but would tip a waiter $100 if they loved the restaurant. Scorpios are so unpredictable, it's almost fun.

SAGITTARIUS

Sagittariuses are very straightforward. You're either on the same page as them or you're not. It's their way or the highway, baby. Their bullshit meter is almost too strong for their own good. Sagittariuses KNOW when you're up to something and they will not let you get away with it. Their jokes are funny and their insults are even better.

CAPRICORN

There is something so mysterious about Capricorns. You may know them, but who are they REALLY?! You can't help but wonder what goes on in their heads. They don't need ANYONE! A Capricorn could spend a week alone and wouldn't even notice because they have so many random interests and are so focused. Low-key Capricorns are meme gods—they always find the best memes.

AQUARIUS

Aquariuses are great to talk to. They like to explore deep topics and always have a lot to add because they are so observant, but BEWARE! DO NOT TALK TO THEM BEFORE THEY'VE HAD THEIR COFFEE!!! Aquariuses do not know how to hide their emotions (especially in the morning; at least that has been my experience). They will sass you so hard that you'll need to lie down for the rest of the day. Despite this attitude, Aquariuses will rarely judge you. You could tell them you just sharted and they would never think differently of you. How great is that?!

PISCES

PISCES! STOP CRYING! EVERYTHING IS GOING TO BE OKAY! Pisces cry while literally watching any movie. It could be a comedy and a Pisces would find a reason to start crying. I feel like Pisces are the real-life version of a romance novel—kinda corny, kinda romantic, and kinda entertaining. But let me tell you, if you are upset, talk to a Pisces. They will cry with you and make you feel so much better.

february

Month

Sunday	Monday	Tuesday	Wednesday
	1 1.6 quiz due -chem cal HW tutoring - 3-4 COVID test - 5:15	2 owl 4 HW due cal HW study for exam!	3 module 3 quiz due -chem cal HW
7 OWL 5 HW due	8 2.2 quiz due -chem	9 owl HW 6 due	10 2.3 quiz due -chem
14 Valentines Day! OWL 8 HW due	15 module 2 quiz due -chem	16	17 3.1 quiz -chem owl 9 HW due
21 owl 9 HW due	22 3.3 quiz -chem	23	24 3.4 quiz owl 11 HW due
28			

2021
Year

Thursday	Friday	Saturday
pre-recital 4 10 hr 2 due - 8:30 Am cal HW brooke's beauty walk	2.1 quiz 5 due - chem	work 6 6-2
owl 7 11 Hw due change Pros-Eng due	2.4 quiz 12 due chem	13
18	3.2 19 quiz due - chem	20
25	(module 26 3 quiz - chem	27

NOTES

February

Month

2021

Year

Notes:

---

1 Monday

Chem 1.6 quiz due

Calculus HW due , tutoring 3-4 ish

Covid test at 5:15

need to run <u>and</u> swim!!

Study for chem test Wednesday

· Class schedule

cal - 8 - 8:50

chem - 10:10 - 11:00

---

2 Tuesday

owl 4 HW due

Calculus HW due

need to run and swim!!

study for chem test!!!

soccer physical - 3:30

Class schedule

cal 8 - 8:50

English - 12:30 - 1:45

---

3 Wednesday

?! module 1 quiz!!! - chem

cal HW

run and swim!!

do pre lab

and pre recitation 2

Class schedule

cal - 8:00 - 8:50

chem - 10:10 - 11

4 Thursday

cal homework
prelab and recitation due
Brooke's beauty walk in Tuscaloosa - 7pm

class schedule

cal - 8 - 8:50
Recitation - 9:30 - 10:20
English - 12:30 - 1:45
Chemlab - 2 - 4:50

5 Friday

2.1 chem quiz due
!! Run and swim !!
go to the fields and practice for
soccer !!

class schedule

Chem - 10:10 - 11
- Engineering - 1:30 - 4
@ (in person) @

6 Saturday

work 6am - 2pm
take a nap
make some pizza and watch netflix or do something
enjoyable

7 Sunday

owl 5 Hwave
cal HW

Month | **Year**

Notes:

○ Monday

_____
_____
_____

_____
_____

○ Tuesday

_____
_____
_____
_____
_____

○ Wednesday

_____
_____
_____
_____
_____

Thursday

Friday

Saturday

Sunday

Month   **Year**

Notes:

Monday

_____
_____
_____
_____
_____
_____

Tuesday

_____
_____
_____
_____
_____
_____

Wednesday

_____
_____
_____
_____
_____

Thursday

Friday

Saturday

Sunday

Try a new hobby today. Try rock climbing or something, IDK.

Month   **Year**

Notes:

Monday

_____
_____
_____
_____
_____
_____

Tuesday

_____
_____
_____
_____
_____
_____

Wednesday

_____
_____
_____
_____
_____

Thursday

Friday

Saturday

Sunday

Month   **Year**

Notes:

Monday

Tuesday

Wednesday

Thursday

Friday

Saturday

Sunday

What am I looking forward to next month?

DOODLE

You can breed any two animals to create your own. What is it?

Design a dress
or an outfit
for a very
fancy
event.

⇥ FASHION ⇤
Would You Rather...?

Wear a bright yellow wig for a month	or	Wear a bright purple wig for a month
Wear a fedora on a first date	or	Wear awkward cargo shorts on a first date
Wear a onesie to a job interview	or	Wear underwear over your pants to a job interview
Wear suspenders every day for the rest of your life	or	Wear the ugliest belt you have ever seen for the rest of your life
Constantly FEEL like you have a wedgie, but nobody can see it	or	Constantly LOOK like you have a wedgie, but you can't feel it
Wear your shoes on the wrong feet to a wedding	or	Wear bedazzled platform flip-flops to a wedding
Wear socks with sandals to a party	or	Wear neon leg warmers to a party
Tuck your jeans into your socks EVERY TIME you wear jeans	or	Always have a huge coffee stain on the front of your shirt
Wear a pair of pants that still has the tag/sticker on it from the store	or	Wear a pair of pants with the fly down

September

Month

Sunday	Monday	Tuesday	Wednesday
20th Bday! 12	realized 13 I probably have ADHD so starting this again	19	

2021

Year

Thursday	Friday	Saturday

NOTES

September   2021

Month   **Year**

Notes: take control of the ADHD

Monday

14 Tuesday

10:00 am - ~~get up~~ and eat	3:30 - workout
10:30 - ~~watch~~ remy	
11:00 play guitar 3 ~~shower~~	5:00 - bathe remy
12:00 - study math	6:30 - shower
1:00 - eat - look at new jobs	7:00 - eat
2:00 - study chem	8:00 read book / guitar

Wednesday

Thursday

Friday

Saturday

Sunday

Month _____ **Year** _____

Notes:

Monday
_____
_____
_____
_____
_____

Tuesday
_____
_____
_____
_____
_____

Wednesday
_____
_____
_____
_____
_____

Thursday

Friday

Saturday

Sunday

| **Month** | **Year** |

Notes:

Monday

_____
_____
_____
_____

_____
_____

Tuesday

_____
_____
_____
_____
_____

Wednesday

_____
_____
_____
_____
_____

Thursday

Friday

Saturday

Sunday

Month _____ **Year** _____

Notes:

_____

Monday

_____
_____
_____

_____
_____

Tuesday

_____
_____
_____
_____
_____

Wednesday

_____
_____
_____
_____
_____

Thursday

Friday

Saturday

Sunday

Month   **Year**

Notes:

Monday

Tuesday

Wednesday

Thursday

Friday

Saturday

Sunday

LIST OF PEOPLE YOU HAVEN'T TALKED TO IN A WHILE

(Maybe you should give them a call.)

_____   _____

_____   _____

_____   _____

_____   _____

_____   _____

_____   _____

_____   _____

LIST OF BAD HABITS TO BREAK

_____   _____

_____   _____

_____   _____

_____   _____

_____   _____

_____   _____

CUSS WORDS · CROSSWORD

WORD BANK

Ass
Asshole
Bitch
Damn
Fuck
Idiot
Loser
Shit
Stupid
Weenie

ACROSS

2

5 The band Green Day has a song called "American _____"

6 Something you might call someone when they cut you off in traffic

9 When I stub my toe, I probably will yell, "_____"

10 A commonly used slang term for "hot dog"

DOWN

1 When your parents get home and you haven't cleaned up your room yet, they will probably shout, "GOD _____ IT"

3 A more inappropriate word for *poop*

4 A word that can describe your best friend, your worst enemy, or a female dog

7 Crazy, _____, love

8 In middle school, bullies would make "L" gestures with their hands and place them against their foreheads to imply you were a _____

COLOR THIS IN:

HOW WAS YOUR DAY? HONESTLY.

Would You Rather...?

Only be able to eat oatmeal for a year	or	Have to eat moldy food every day for a week
Win $10 million but not be able to spend it for fifty years	or	Win $1 million that you can spend immediately
Be completely alone for a year	or	Have to spend a whole year with people who piss you off
Feel sunburned for the rest of your life	or	Feel the pain of childbirth for a week
Have fifteen kids	or	Have no kids at all
Get a papercut on your eyeball	or	Cut all your toenails *wayyyy* too short
Never be able to look in a mirror again	or	Never be allowed to see a photo of yourself again
Show your entire camera roll to your family	or	Show your entire internet history to your family
Be able to read minds	or	Simply not be able to read minds (Personally, I would NOT want to)
Be an extremely fast runner	or	Be an Olympic gymnast

LIST OF PET PEEVES

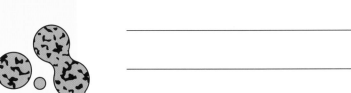

IF YOU COULD START A BUSINESS, WHAT WOULD IT BE?

YOUR FUTURE

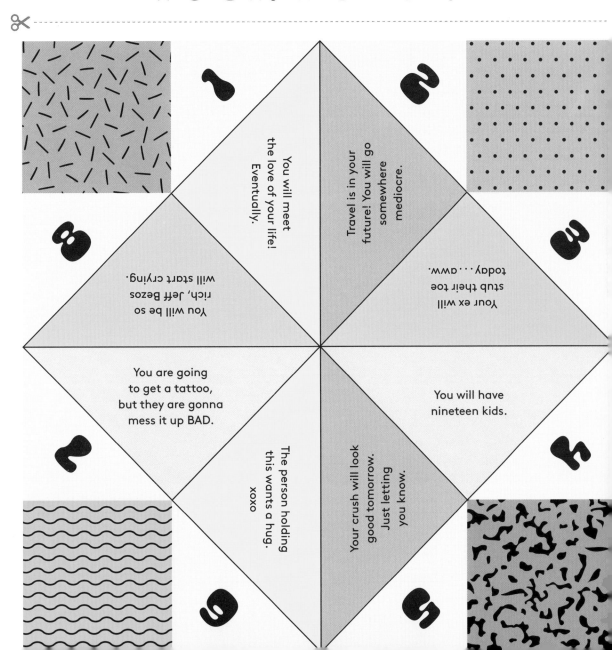

1

You will meet the love of your life! Eventually.

2

Travel is in your future! You will go somewhere mediocre.

8

You will be so rich, Jeff Bezos will start crying.

3

Your ex will stub their toe today . . . aww.

You are going to get a tattoo, but they are gonna mess it up BAD.

You will have nineteen kids.

7

The person holding this wants a hug. xoxo

Your crush will look good tomorrow. Just letting you know.

6

5

MAKE

1. Cut around the outside of the Cootie Catcher.

2. Fold in half and then fold in half again.

3. Open out, turn the paper over (writing side down), and fold each corner into the middle.

4. Turn over and repeat.

5. Fold bottom half up and work fingers into pockets.

PLAY

1. One player holds the Cootie Catcher open, while the other player picks a color. The player holding the game spells the color, letter by letter, as they close and then open it.

2. The other player then picks a number. The player holding the game closes and then opens it that number of times.

3. The other player then picks a second number. This time, the player holding the game lifts the flap to reveal the other player's fortune.

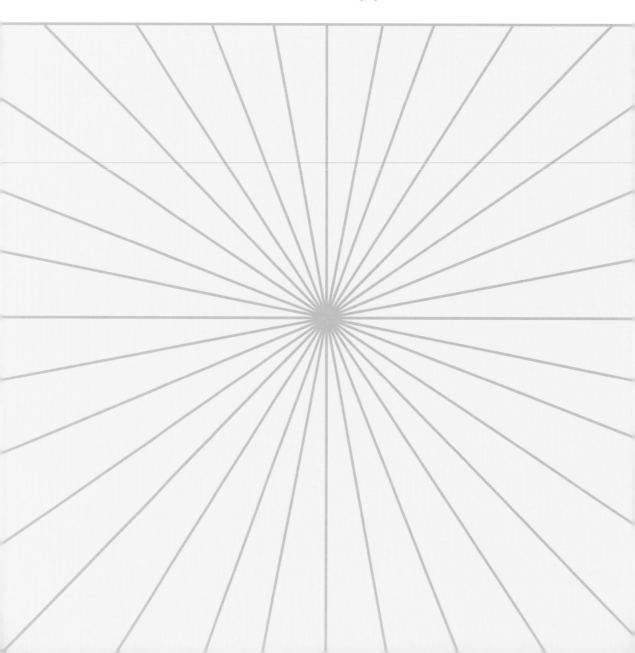

COOTIES

COOTIES

COOTIES

COOTIES

COOTIES

Month

Sunday	Monday	Tuesday	Wednesday

Year

Thursday	Friday	Saturday

NOTES

Month | **Year**

Notes:

⬤ Monday

_____
_____
_____
_____
_____
_____

⬤ Tuesday

_____
_____
_____
_____
_____

⬤ Wednesday

_____
_____
_____
_____
_____

Thursday

Friday

Saturday

Sunday

Month | **Year**

Notes:

● Monday

_____

Remember to drink water today.

● Tuesday

● Wednesday

Thursday

Friday

Saturday

Sunday

Month

Year

Notes:

Monday

_____
_____
_____
_____
_____

Tuesday

_____
_____
_____
_____
_____
_____

Wednesday

_____
_____
_____
_____
_____
_____

Thursday

Friday

Saturday

Sunday

Month | **Year**

Notes:

Monday
_____
_____
_____
_____

_____
_____

Tuesday
_____
_____
_____
_____
_____
_____

Wednesday
_____
_____
_____
_____
_____

Thursday

Friday

Saturday

Sunday

Month	**Year**

Notes:

Monday

Tuesday

Wednesday

Thursday

Friday

Saturday

Sunday

DRAW
SOMETHING
SCARY.

QUOTES ARE SO CORNY.

(But write down some of your favorites.)

GOALS FOR THE MONTH
GOALS FOR THE MONTH
GOALS FOR THE MONTH
GOALS FOR THE MONTH

e.g., This month I am going to talk to someone other than my cat.

-
-
-
-
-
-
-
-
-
-
-
-
-
-

SKETCH

TATTOO

IDEAS

BODY PARTS

Armpit ~~Eyelid~~ ~~Cuticle~~ ~~Foot~~ ~~Elbow~~

Knee   Neck   ~~Mouth~~   ~~Ear~~   ~~Nose~~   ~~Nail~~

```
O  O  C  E  N  T  T  L  R  L  N  D  K  K
I  A  O  U  I  T  E  Y  C  M  S  I  N  W
W  N  T  N  T  C  R  N  L  S  C  L  E  T
W  A  A  M  I  I  K  E  R  E  F  E  E  N
M  N  O  I  O  E  C  S  M  R  O  Y  E  O
U  E  E  N  L  E  U  L  M  T  S  E  K  O
O  O  L  O  E  O  E  I  E  E  U  N  K  L
H  T  B  S  I  E  L  T  N  O  E  M  P  L
O  T  O  E  C  T  A  M  I  N  L  P  C  N
O  A  W  N  A  T  B  R  I  N  E  L  O  E
T  L  T  C  O  L  O  A  R  M  P  I  T  T
I  O  A  A  L  N  E  C  K  L  T  I  N  L
E  E  O  M  O  U  T  H  S  L  O  F  I  U
K  E  I  F  O  K  N  W  C  I  O  E  N  H
```

Month

Sunday	Monday	Tuesday	Wednesday

Year

Thursday	Friday	Saturday

Month

Year

Notes:

○ Monday

○ Tuesday

○ Wednesday

Thursday

Friday

Saturday

Sunday

Month	Year

Notes:

○ Monday

_____

_____

_____

_____

_____

_____

○ Tuesday

_____

_____

_____

_____

_____

_____

○ Wednesday

_____

_____

_____

_____

_____

Thursday

Friday

Saturday

Sunday

Month   **Year**

Notes:

Monday

Tuesday

Wednesday

Thursday

Friday

Saturday

Sunday

Month | **Year**

Notes:

Monday
_____
_____
_____
_____

_____
_____

Tuesday
_____
_____
_____
_____
_____
_____

Wednesday
_____
_____
_____
_____
_____

Thursday

Tell someone you love them.

Friday

Saturday

Sunday

Month   **Year**

Notes:

Monday

_____

_____

_____

_____

_____

Tuesday

_____

_____

_____

_____

_____

Wednesday

_____

_____

_____

_____

_____

Thursday

Friday

Saturday

Sunday

Write down the playlist of your life.

_____ Artist   _____ Song

_____ Artist   _____ Song

_____ Artist   _____ Song

_____ Artist   _____ Song

_____ Artist   _____ Song

_____ Artist   _____ Song

_____ Artist   _____ Song

_____ Artist   _____ Song

_____ Artist   _____ Song

_____ Artist   _____ Song

Have you ever had an argument
with someone and later thought,

I could have said something so
much better? Write that down here.

DESIGN A MAGAZINE COVER
WITH YOU ON THE FRONT.

WRITE A REVIEW ABOUT THE LAST RESTAURANT THAT DID YOU DIRTY.

→ _____

☆ ☆ ☆ ☆ ☆

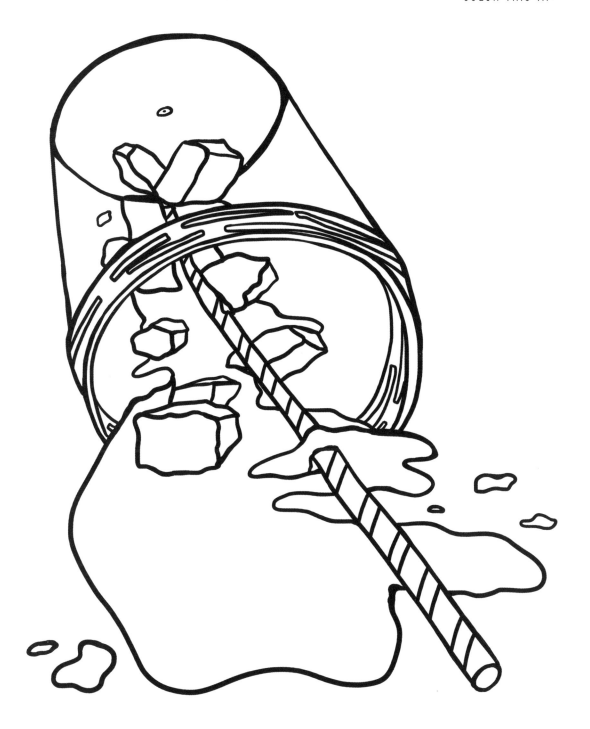

Month

Sunday	Monday	Tuesday	Wednesday

Year

Thursday	Friday	Saturday

Month | **Year**

Notes:

Monday

Tuesday

Wednesday

Thursday

Friday

Saturday

Sunday

Month	Year

Notes:

Monday

_____

_____

_____

_____

Tuesday

_____

_____

_____

_____

_____

Wednesday

_____

_____

_____

_____

_____

Thursday

Friday

Saturday

Sunday

Month　　　　　　　**Year**

Notes:

○ Monday

_____
_____
_____
_____
_____
_____

○ Tuesday

_____
_____
_____
_____
_____
_____

○ Wednesday

_____
_____
_____
_____
_____
_____

Thursday

Friday

Saturday

Sunday

Month   **Year**

Notes:

Monday

Tuesday

Wednesday

Thursday

Friday

Saturday

Sunday

Month

Year

Notes:

Monday

Tuesday

Wednesday

Go to bed early. It's good for you.

Thursday

Friday

Saturday

Sunday

WHAT DO YOU THINK ALIENS

LOOK LIKE? SKETCH IDEAS.

ANALYZE ONE OF YOUR DREAMS.

What do you think it meant?

Write down something you have never told anyone . . . ever.

_____

_____

_____

_____

_____

_____

_____

_____

Whether it's small or big, we all have something.

DRAW A CARTOON VERSION OF YOURSELF.

Month

Sunday	Monday	Tuesday	Wednesday

Year

Thursday	Friday	Saturday

Month   **Year**

Notes:

Monday

_____
_____
_____
_____

_____
_____

Tuesday

_____
_____
_____
_____
_____
_____

Wednesday

_____
_____
_____
_____
_____

Thursday

Friday

Saturday

Sunday

Month   **Year**

Notes:

Monday

Tuesday

Wednesday

Thursday

Friday

Saturday

Sunday

Month

Year

Notes:

Monday

Tuesday

Wednesday

Thursday

Friday

Saturday

Sunday

Month | **Year**

Notes:

Monday

_____

_____

_____

_____

_____

_____

Tuesday

_____

_____

_____

_____

_____

_____

Wednesday

_____

_____

_____

_____

_____

_____

Thursday

Friday

Saturday

Sunday

Month **Year**

Notes:

Monday

Tuesday

Wednesday

Thursday

Friday

Saturday

Sunday

RAWR!

PARTY ANIMAL

Plan your next birthday party . . .
or if you're like me and hate birthdays, plan someone else's.

WHO

WHAT

WHEN

WHERE

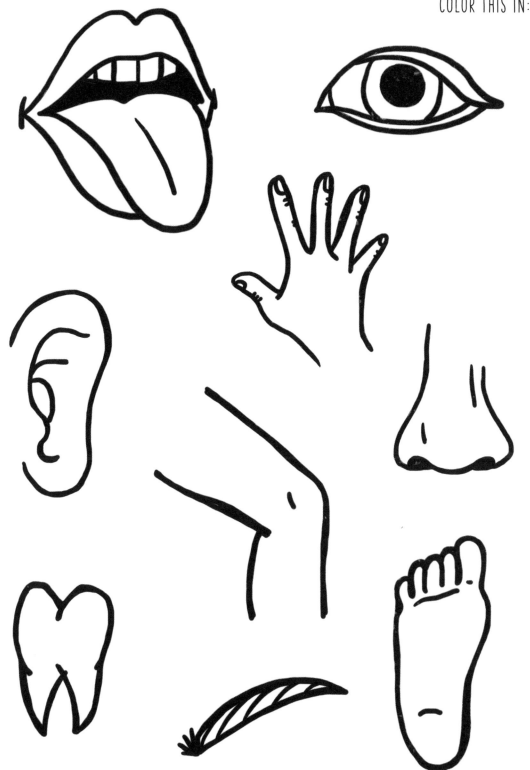

Date _____

Dear _____

_____

_____

_____

_____

_____

_____

_____

_____

_____

_____

_____

_____

_____

_____

_____

WRITE A

LETTER

TO YOUR

CURRENT

CRUSH.

Personally, I hate having crushes
on people . . . and I especially
hate interacting with them . . .
so this is a nice alternative.

Dates are bullshit overall.

But if you HAD to go on one, what would you do?
Describe your ideal date.

Month

Sunday	Monday	Tuesday	Wednesday

Year

Thursday	Friday	Saturday

Month   **Year**

Notes:

Monday

_____

_____

_____

_____

_____

Tuesday

_____

_____

_____

_____

_____

Cook yourself something special for dinner.

Wednesday

_____

_____

_____

_____

_____

Thursday

Friday

Saturday

Sunday

Month

Year

Notes:

Monday
_____
_____
_____

Tuesday
_____
_____
_____
_____
_____

Wednesday
_____
_____
_____
_____
_____

Thursday

Friday

Saturday

Sunday

Month   **Year**

Notes:

Monday

Tuesday

Wednesday

Thursday

Friday

Saturday

Sunday

Month

Year

Notes:

Monday

Tuesday

Wednesday

Thursday

Friday

Saturday

Sunday

Month   **Year**

Notes:

Monday

Tuesday

Wednesday

Thursday

Friday

Saturday

Sunday

WRITE A LETTER TO YOUR FUTURE CHILD.

Date _____

Dear _____

_____

_____

||| _____

_____ |||

_____

_____

_____

_____

_____

_____

_____

_____

_____

_____

_____

Draw a picture of what you think your baby is going to look like.

DRAW A CAR THAT DOESN'T EXIST.*

*Be a little like Elon Musk.

What do you love about yourself?

Make a list. Not to get deep here, but self-reflection can feel really good.

_____ _____

_____ _____

_____ _____

_____ _____

_____ _____

_____ _____

_____ _____

_____ _____

_____ _____

_____ _____

_____ _____

Plan a fun day for you and your friends.

- _____
- _____
- _____
- _____
- _____
- _____
- _____
- _____
- _____
- _____
- _____
- _____
- _____

DRAW A PICTURE OF YOUR PET.

Month

Sunday	Monday	Tuesday	Wednesday

Year

Thursday	Friday	Saturday

Month

Year

Notes:

Monday

_____

Tuesday

_____

Wednesday

_____

Thursday

Friday

Saturday

Sunday

Month	**Year**

Notes:

Monday

_____
_____
_____
_____
_____

Tuesday

_____
_____
_____
_____
_____

Wednesday

_____
_____
_____
_____

Thursday

Friday

Saturday

Sunday

Month

Year

Notes:

Monday

_____
_____
_____
_____
_____
_____

Tuesday

_____
_____
_____
_____
_____
_____

Wednesday

_____
_____
_____
_____
_____
_____

Thursday

Friday

Saturday

Put your phone down and go watch the sunset or something.

Sunday

Month   **Year**

Notes:

Monday

_____
_____
_____
_____
_____
_____

Tuesday

_____
_____
_____
_____
_____
_____

Wednesday

_____
_____
_____
_____
_____

Thursday

Friday

Saturday

Sunday

Month	**Year**

Notes:

Monday

_____
_____
_____
_____
_____
_____

Tuesday

_____
_____
_____
_____
_____
_____

Wednesday

_____
_____
_____
_____
_____
_____

Thursday

Friday

Saturday

Sunday

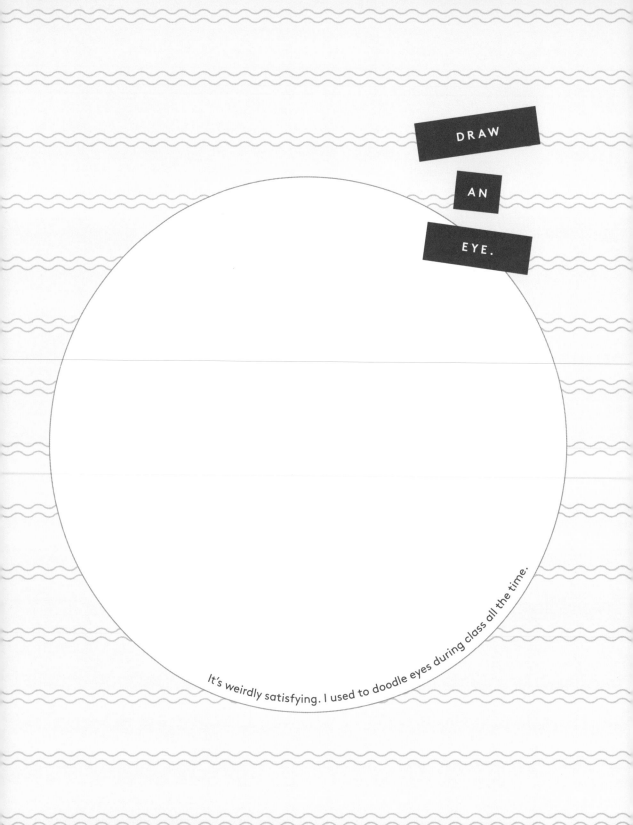

DRAW

AN

EYE.

It's weirdly satisfying. I used to doodle eyes during class all the time.

DRAW A PICTURE OF

A YUMMY MEAL.

SWIPE RIGHT

Write bios for your friends' dating profiles.

_____
Name

_____
Age

_____
Location

_____
Guilty pleasure

_____
Song that describes me

_____
Favorite food

_____
What I like in a partner

_____
Hobbies

_____
Weird fact about me

_____
Name

_____
Age

_____
Location

_____
Guilty pleasure

_____
Song that describes me

_____
Favorite food

_____
What I like in a partner

_____
Hobbies

_____
Weird fact about me

_____
Name

_____
Age

_____
Location

_____
Guilty pleasure

_____
Song that describes me

_____
Favorite food

_____
What I like in a partner

_____
Hobbies

_____
Weird fact about me

DRAW YOUR DREAM HOUSE.

Month

Sunday	Monday	Tuesday	Wednesday

Year

Thursday	Friday	Saturday

NOTES

Month   **Year**

Notes:

○ Monday

○ Tuesday

○ Wednesday

Thursday

Friday

Saturday

Sunday

Month   **Year**

Notes:

Monday

_____
_____
_____
_____
_____

Tuesday

_____
_____
_____
_____
_____

Wednesday

_____
_____
_____
_____
_____

Thursday

Friday

Saturday

Sunday

Month	**Year**

Notes:

Monday

Tuesday

Wednesday

Thursday

Friday

Saturday

Sunday

Month   **Year**

Notes:

Monday

_____
_____
_____
_____
_____

Tuesday

_____
_____
_____
_____
_____

Wednesday

_____
_____
_____
_____
_____

Thursday

Friday

Saturday

Sunday

Month   **Year**

Notes:

Monday

_____
_____
_____
_____
_____

Tuesday

_____
_____
_____
_____
_____
_____

Wednesday

_____
_____
_____
_____
_____

Thursday

Friday

Saturday

Sunday

WHAT'S SOMETHING YOU WANT REALLY FUCKING BAD?

→ _____

Now, come up with a plan on how you're going to get it.

_____

_____

_____

_____

_____

_____

_____

_____

_____

_____

_____

_____

_____

_____

LIST FIVE NEW THINGS YOU WANT TO TRY OR HAVE ALWAYS WANTED TO TRY.

Whenever I'm going through a tough time I make a list
like this. It gives me something to look forward to.

VENT ABOUT

SOMETHING THAT IS BOTHERING YOU.

_____

_____

_____

_____

_____

_____

_____

_____

_____

_____

_____

_____

_____

_____

_____

_____

_____

_____

_____

_____

You wake

up with

$1 million—

what do you

do with it?

Month

Sunday	Monday	Tuesday	Wednesday

Year

Thursday	Friday	Saturday

NOTES

Month	**Year**

Notes:

Monday

Tuesday

Wednesday

Thursday

Friday

Saturday

Sunday

Month   **Year**

Notes:

Monday

_____
_____
_____
_____
_____
_____

Tuesday

_____
_____
_____
_____
_____

Wednesday

_____
_____
_____
_____
_____

Thursday

Friday

Saturday

Sunday

Month

Year

Notes:

○ Monday

Treat yourself to a coffee.

○ Tuesday

○ Wednesday

Thursday

Friday

Saturday

Sunday

Month _____   **Year** _____

Notes:

Monday

_____
_____
_____
_____
_____

Tuesday

_____
_____
_____
_____
_____

Wednesday

_____
_____
_____
_____
_____

Thursday

Friday

Saturday

Sunday

Month

Year

Notes:

Monday

Tuesday

Wednesday

Thursday

Friday

Saturday

Sunday

Draw
yourself
as a
superhero.

Come up with
an epic movie plot.

_____

_____

_____

_____

_____

_____

_____

_____

_____

_____

_____

_____

_____

_____

_____

_____

PLAN A PRANK.

- _____
- _____
- _____
- _____
- _____
- _____
- _____
- _____
- _____
- _____
- _____
- _____
- _____

WRITE DOWN WHATEVER THE FUCK YOU WANT.

WHERE

I

HAVE

BEEN.

WHERE I WANT TO GO.

Month

Sunday	Monday	Tuesday	Wednesday

Year

Thursday	Friday	Saturday

NOTES

Month   **Year**

Notes:

Monday

_____
_____
_____
_____

_____

Tuesday

_____
_____
_____
_____
_____

Wednesday

_____
_____
_____
_____
_____

Thursday

Friday

Compliment someone who needs it. We all have those days.

Saturday

Sunday

Month   **Year**

Notes: _____

Monday

Tuesday

Wednesday

Thursday

Friday

Saturday

Sunday

Month | **Year**

Notes:

Monday

_____
_____
_____
_____
_____

Tuesday

_____
_____
_____
_____
_____

Wednesday

_____
_____
_____
_____
_____

Thursday

Friday

Saturday

Sunday

Month   **Year**

Notes:

Monday

_____
_____
_____
_____
_____
_____

Tuesday

_____
_____
_____
_____
_____
_____

Wednesday

_____
_____
_____
_____
_____

Thursday

Friday

Saturday

Sunday

Month   **Year**

Notes:

Monday

_____

Tuesday

_____

Wednesday

Thursday

Friday

Saturday

Sunday

COLOR THIS IN:

WRITE A POEM ABOUT SOMETHING RANDOM.

I used to love writing poems in
middle school. Why not try it again?

**WHEN I DRINK COFFEE
I FEEL GREAT
IT MAKES ME FEEL LIKE
I AM SWIMMING IN A LAKE**

(That did not rhyme or make sense. Sorry. . . .)

_____

_____

_____

_____

_____

_____

_____

_____

_____

DRAW YOUR FAVORITE PLACE
(IT'S OKAY IF IT'S YOUR BED).

Aesthetic

Make the most aEsTheTic mood board.
Cut out pictures from a magazine, or print stuff out, or do whatever you want!

Everything That Makes Me Smile

Make a mood board of things you love.
Cut out pictures from a magazine, or print stuff out, or do whatever you want!

Name _____   Social _____

Phone _____   Social _____

Email _____   Social _____
~~~~~~~~~~~~~~~~~~~~~~~~~~~~~~~~

Name _____   Social _____

Phone _____   Social _____

Email _____   Social _____
~~~~~~~~~~~~~~~~~~~~~~~~~~~~~~~~

Name _____   Social _____

Phone _____   Social _____

Email _____   Social _____
~~~~~~~~~~~~~~~~~~~~~~~~~~~~~~~~

Name _____   Social _____

Phone _____   Social _____

Email _____   Social _____
~~~~~~~~~~~~~~~~~~~~~~~~~~~~~~~~

Name _____   Social _____

Phone _____   Social _____

Email _____   Social _____
~~~~~~~~~~~~~~~~~~~~~~~~~~~~~~~~

IMPORTANT CONTACTS (just in case)

Name

Social

Phone

Social

Email

Social

Name

Social

Phone

Social

Email

Social

Name

Social

Phone

Social

Email

Social

Name

Social

Phone

Social

Email

Social

Name

Social

Phone

Social

Email

Social

Name _____

Phone _____

Email _____
~~~~~~~~~~~~~~~~~~~~~~~~~~~~~~~~~~~

Name _____

Phone _____

Email _____
~~~~~~~~~~~~~~~~~~~~~~~~~~~~~~~~~~~

Name _____

Phone _____

Email _____
~~~~~~~~~~~~~~~~~~~~~~~~~~~~~~~~~~~

Name _____

Phone _____

Email _____
~~~~~~~~~~~~~~~~~~~~~~~~~~~~~~~~~~~

Name _____

Phone _____

Email _____
~~~~~~~~~~~~~~~~~~~~~~~~~~~~~~~~~~~

Social _____

Social _____

Social _____

Social _____

Social _____

Social _____

Social _____

Social _____

Social _____

Social _____

Social _____

Social _____

Social _____

Social _____

Social _____

IMPORTANT CONTACTS (just in case)

PASSWORDS

(KEEP THIS CONFIDENTIAL!)

Website	Username	Password

notes

WOW! CONGRATULATIONS!
You finished the planner! This is not something that's easy to stick to, so you should feel very accomplished. I hope that using this planner helped you form new good habits (and that you had fun using it, too, of course). I appreciate every single one of you who decided to give this planner a chance.
I love you all very much!

-Emma